# FREE GIFT

As a token of gratitude, I've prepared a special gift for our little ones. Enjoy cute coloring pages with self-love affirmations, designed especially for little girls of Asian heritage.

Download your printable file here:

UpflyBooks.com/free

Dream big, our little Boo
— Mommy & Daddy —

Copyright © 2023 by Yeonsil Yoo.

All rights reserved. No part of this book may be reproduced or transmitted
in any form or by any means, electronic or mechanical, including photocopying,
recording, or by any information storage and retrieval system,
without prior written permission from the copyright holder.

www.upflybooks.com

Paperback: 978-1-7388188-7-7
eBook PDF: 978-1-7388188-8-4
Hardcover: 978-1-7389124-4-5

My First Trip to China
我的第一次中国之旅

Made with ❤ by Upfly Books

Written by Yeonsil Yoo | Illustrated by Anastasiya Halionka | Translated by Lucy YuTing Chu

"Yay! School is over!"
"耶!学期结束了!"

Summer vacation has started at Ying Ying's school.
颖颖学校的暑假开始了。

Ying Ying is excited to play with her favorite toys every day at home.
颖颖很期待每天在家玩她最喜欢的玩具。

"Do you like summer vacation?" Mommy asks.
"你喜欢放暑假吗?"妈妈问道。

"Yeah! Vacation is the best!"
"喜欢呀!放假最棒了!"

"Why do you like vacation? What do you want to do?"
Mommy looks at Ying Ying curiously.
"你为什么喜欢放假?你想做些什么呢?"
妈妈好奇地看着颖颖。

Every day I can watch TV,
我可以每天看电视、

eat ice cream,
吃冰淇淋、

and play with Fishy and T-rex!
然后跟大眼鱼和暴龙玩!

Oh, and Ducky as well!
哦、还有黄色小鸭!

"But Ying Ying, you can play with your toys any time.
This summer, why don't we go to China?
"但是颖颖,你什么时候都可以跟你的玩具们玩呀、
要不我们这个暑假去中国吧?

You can try a summer camp in China and meet new friends there!"
你可以尝试一下中国的夏令营然后认识那里的新朋友!"

"No! I don't want new friends!" Ying Ying shouts.
"不!我不要新朋友!"颖颖喊道。

"Then, what about visiting Grandma and Grandpa? If we go to China, we can visit and play with Grandma, Grandpa, Aunt, and Uncle." Mommy talks softly while she holds Ying Ying's hands.

"那去看奶奶和爷爷呢？如果我们去中国、我们就可以去找奶奶、爷爷、阿姨和叔叔玩。"
妈妈握着颖颖的手、温柔地说道。

"I miss Grandma and Grandpa…"
"我想奶奶和爷爷…"

Ying Ying wants to visit and play with Grandma, Grandpa, Aunt, and Uncle, but she doesn't want to make new friends.

颖颖想要找奶奶、爷爷、阿姨和叔叔玩、但是她不想交新朋友。

On the plane to China, Ying Ying looks out the window.
在前往中国的飞机上、颖颖看向窗外。

Big, fluffy clouds are everywhere,
and all the houses and cars under the clouds look so tiny.
They look like her toys at home.
到处都是又大又蓬松的云、
云底下的所有房子和车子看起来都好迷你、
它们看起来就像她家里的玩具。

But she can't stop thinking about the camp in China
Mommy was talking about.
但她一直忍不住去想
妈妈之前所说的中国夏令营。

'What if no one wants to play with me?'
'如果没有人想跟我玩怎么办?'

'I can't speak Chinese well. What if the other kids make fun of me?
I just want to stay at home and watch TV every day!'
'我中文说得不好。如果其他小朋友嘲笑我怎么办?
我只想要待在家然后每天看电视!'

After a long flight, the plane lands in China.
在漫长的飞行后、飞机在中国降落了。

At the airport, Grandma, Grandpa, Aunt, and Uncle
welcome Ying Ying with big hugs.
在机场，奶奶、爷爷、阿姨和叔叔
用大大的拥抱迎接颖颖。

Although Ying Ying has chatted with them through video calls so many times,
she is too shy to say "Ni Hao" ("hello" in Chinese).
So she just hides behind Mommy.
尽管颖颖已经跟他们视频通话过很多次了、
她还是不好意思说"你好"。所以她只躲在妈妈身后。

Aunt and Uncle give Ying Ying lots of toys, and Grandma and Grandpa spoil her with so many yummy ice creams and snacks.
Ying Ying is so happy with all of these gifts and goodies.
阿姨和叔叔送给颖颖很多玩具、然后爷爷和奶奶也为她准备了好多好吃的冰激凌和点心。
颖颖好喜欢这些礼物和好吃的东西。

"Is it delicious, Ying Ying?" Grandma asks.
"好吃吗、颖颖?" 奶奶问道。

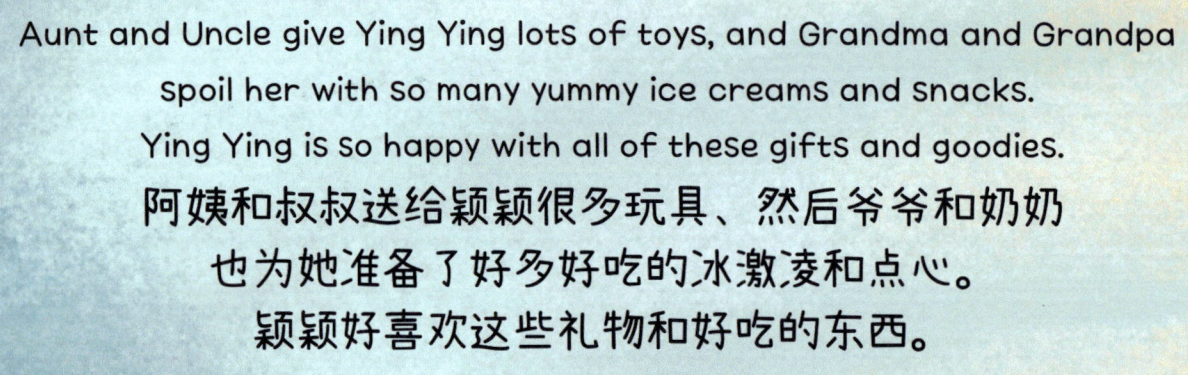

"Yeah, it's so yummy! I love ice cream! But Grandma, don't tell Mommy! Mommy said I shouldn't eat too much ice cream!"
Ying Ying speaks in a whispering voice to Grandma.
"嗯、好好吃!我爱冰淇淋!但是奶奶,不要跟妈妈说!妈妈说我不能吃太多冰淇淋!"
颖颖悄悄地对奶奶说。

"Okay, this is our secret!" Grandma says, with a big smile.
"好、这是我们的秘密!"奶奶带着大大的笑容说道。

Ying Ying slowly decides that she will like visiting China.
颖颖慢慢开始觉得她会喜欢她的中国之旅。

But whenever Mommy talks about the summer camp,
Ying Ying becomes worried.
但是每当妈妈提到夏令营时、
颖颖就开始担心。

"Ying Ying, we're going to visit the new camp tomorrow.
There will be lots of games to play, fun books and toys!
And you can make new friends and meet the teachers!"
Mommy seems excited, but Ying Ying is upset.
"颖颖、我们明天就要去新的夏令营了。
那里会有很多好玩的游戏、书和玩具、
然后你可以交新朋友和认识老师们！"
妈妈看起来很兴奋、但是颖颖很沮丧！

"I told you, I don't wanna go to the new camp!" Ying Ying shouts.
"我跟你说过了、我不想去新的夏令营!"颖颖喊道。

"Why not?"
"为什么不想?"

"If I go to the camp, T-rex will be alone at Grandma's house.
I'm going to stay home and play with T-rex!"
Ying Ying looks down at the floor, trying to hold back her tears.
"因为如果我去夏令营、暴龙就会自己孤单留在奶奶家。
我要待在家跟暴龙玩!"
颖颖看着地上、试着忍住她的眼泪。

"T-rex won't be alone. Mommy will be there with him."
Mommy talks gently to Ying Ying while she rubs Ying Ying's back.
"暴龙不会孤单的、妈妈会陪着他。"
妈妈拍着颖颖的背、轻声说道。

"No! I don't like it! I don't like the camp and the new friends!" Ying Ying cries.
"不要！我不喜欢！我不喜欢那个夏令营和新朋友！"颖颖大声说道。

Mommy scooches down and holds Ying Ying's hands to comfort her.
妈妈蹲下来然后握住颖颖的手来安慰她。

"Ying Ying, we haven't even tried yet, right?
If you don't like it after you try it tomorrow,
you don't have to go anymore.
But you need to at least give it a try. Deal?"
"颖颖、我们连试都还没试过、对吧？
如果你明天试了之后发现不喜欢、
你就不用再去了。
但是你至少要试试看。可以吗？"

"Okay..." Ying Ying reluctantly nods.
"好吧..."颖颖不情愿地点点头。

Finally, it is the first day of summer camp.
终于、夏令营的第一天到来了。

Ying Ying drags herself around the entire morning,
hoping to avoid going to the camp.
颖颖一整个早上都在拖拖拉拉、
希望可以不用去夏令营。

"Ying Ying, you should hurry up and change your clothes!"
"颖颖、你应该抓紧换衣服了！"

"Okay…"
"好吧…"

Ying Ying answers reluctantly,
but she is still rolling around the floor, doing nothing.
颖颖不情愿地回答、
但是她仍然在地上打着滚、什么也不做。

Soon, Mommy enters her room.
不久后、妈妈来到她的房间。

"Ying Ying, you haven't changed yet?
Can you change your clothes, please, right now?"
Mommy is very upset.
"颖颖、你还没换好衣服吗？
可以请你现在去换衣服吗？"妈妈很不开心。

"Okay... I'm changing..."
"好吧...我在换了..."

Ying Ying sighs and starts to change her clothes, one piece at a time.
颖颖叹了口气、然后开始一件一件地换衣服。

Mommy, Daddy, and Ying Ying arrive at the school.
One teacher greets them with a big smile.
妈妈、爸爸和颖颖到达学校。
一位老师用一个大大的笑容向他们打招呼。

"You must be Ying Ying. Welcome to our class!"
"你就是颖颖吧！欢迎来到我们班！"

Ying Ying becomes even more nervous:
unlike back home in Canada, everyone here is speaking only Chinese.
颖颖变得更紧张了。
跟加拿大家乡不同、在这大家都只说中文。

But the teacher continues talking.
"Let's say bye-bye to Mommy and Daddy,
and then I'll introduce you to the other kids in the class!"
但是老师继续说道、
"我们跟妈妈和爸爸说再见吧、
然后我会带你认识班上的其他小朋友！"

Ying Ying sends Mommy and Daddy a signal by shaking her head subtly,
but Mommy and Daddy don't seem to notice.
颖颖偷偷摇了摇头、想给妈妈和爸爸一个暗示、
但是妈妈和爸爸似乎没有发现。

"Have fun!" Mommy and Daddy cheer.
"好好玩哦！"妈妈和爸爸鼓励道。

In the classroom, some of the kids are already chatting, laughing, and running around.

在教室里、有一些小朋友已经开始聊天、嘻笑、到处奔跑。

When Ying Ying enters the classroom, everyone looks at her. Ying Ying tries not to look at anybody.

当颖颖进到教室时、大家都看着她。颖颖试着不看向任何人。

She walks towards some of the toys and picks up a yellow digger toy.

她走向一些玩具然后捡起了一个黄色挖土机玩具。

Her classmates want to talk to her, but no one is willing to be the first one.
她的同学想要和她说话、但是没有人愿意当第一个。

Then, one boy walks over to Ying Ying.
接着、有一个男孩走向颖颖。

"Hi, my name is Hao Hao. What's your name?"
"你好，我的名字是浩浩。你叫什么名字？"

"I'm Ying Ying."
"我是颖颖。"

Hao Hao beams with joy and continues to talk to Ying Ying.
浩浩开心地笑了继续和颖颖说话。

"Do you like diggers? I like them, too!
There's a big yellow digger toy at the play center.
Do you want to go and play together?"
"你喜欢挖土机吗？我也喜欢！
在游戏室有一个很大的黄色挖土机玩具。
你想要一起去玩吗？"

"YEAH!"
"要！"

Ying Ying and Hao Hao hold hands, and together they run to the play center.
颖颖和浩浩牵着手、一起跑向游戏室。

And just like Hao Hao said, there was a big, yellow digger toy in the play center.
果然跟浩浩说的一样、
游戏室有一个很大的黄色挖土机玩具。

"Let's go! Let's hop on it together!"
"走吧！我们一起跳上去！"

Ying Ying and Hao Hao run to the digger.
颖颖和浩浩跑向挖土机。

While she was having so much fun playing with Hao Hao, Ying Ying thought to herself,
当颖颖和浩浩玩得非常开心时、颖颖心想、

'Playing with Hao Hao is so much fun! I can't wait to come back tomorrow!'
'跟浩浩玩真是太好玩了！
我等不及明天再回来了！'

Have you ever been worried or scared about something, before you even tried it?

你有在尝试一件事之前感到担心或害怕过吗？

Sometimes we can be scared of places we've never been, and people who are very different.

有时候我们会害怕我们没去过的地方、和跟我们很不一样的人。

But when we get to know them,
we find out that there is nothing to be scared or worried about.

但是当我们认识他们后、
我们会发现没有什么好害怕或担心的。

So, next time you are scared about something new,
why don't you give it a try first, and see what happens?

所以，下一次当你对新事物感到害怕时、
不妨先试试看、然后看看会发生什么呢？

ABOUT THE AUTHOR

Yeonsil Yoo is a children's author and the proud mother of a multicultural child, Yoona, who is Korean, Chinese, American, and Canadian.

As a mother and entrepreneur, Yeonsil loves to teach her daughter not only about her Asian roots but also vital real-world lessons, particularly in growth mindset, empathy, and tenacity. All of her books aim to share important messages in life with her daughter and other curious young minds. If you'd like to receive her next latest ebook for FREE, please sign up as a beta reader at upflybooks.com.

Explore More Books by the Author

If you loved this book, you're in for more treats! Check out these other amazing books by Yeonsil, each crafted with the same love and care. Find the one that speaks to you:

🛒 **Now Available on Amazon!**

Bilingual
Chinese-English
Picture Book

AGES 5-8

Non-fiction on
World Economy
and History

AGES 8-12

Hope you and your little one enjoyed our story! If so, could you spare a moment to rate the book or share your thoughts on Amazon?

Even a quick one-click rating would mean the world to me. It helps me continue creating more educational and fun stories for awesome kids like yours.

Warm regards,
Yeonsil

P.S. Don't forget your free coloring + writing book:
upflybooks.com/free

Made in United States
Troutdale, OR
07/05/2024